BEAVER BOOKS

My First Bilingual Book • Mon premier livre bilingue

At the Beach

• ◆ •

À la plage

English-French • Français-anglais

— A child's first book of words and fun – in two languages! —
— Un livre bilingue, rempli de mots et de plaisir pour les tout-petits ! —

waves

des vagues

sandcastle

un château de sable

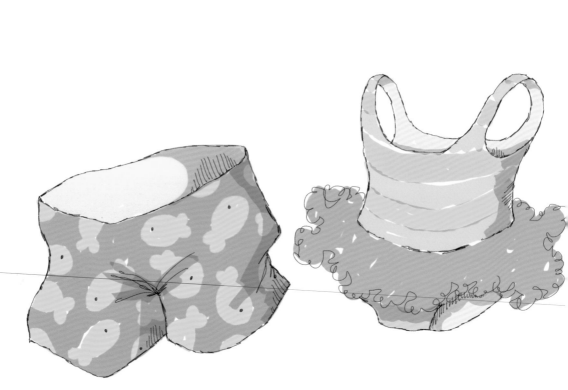

bathing suits

des maillots de bain

umbrella

un parasol

shells

des coquillages

kite

un cerf-volant

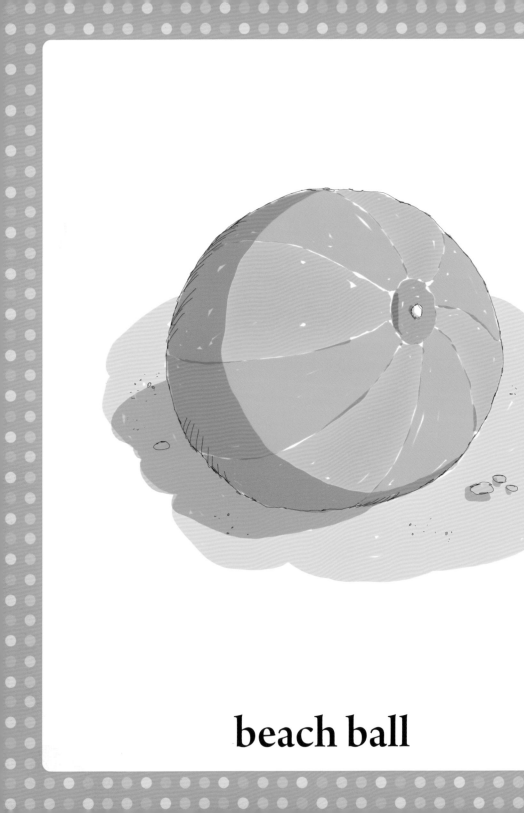

beach ball

un ballon de plage

sunglasses

des lunettes de soleil

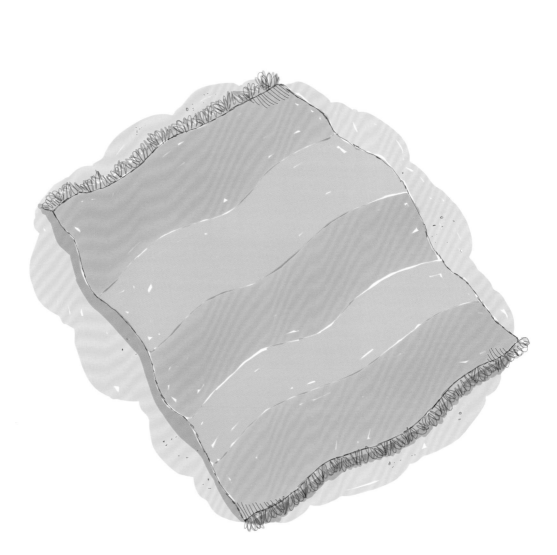

towel

une serviette

seagull

un goéland

ice cream

de la crème glacée

— Fun activities with things at the beach! —
— Des activités amusantes ! —

Can you say the names of these things at the beach, in both French and English?
Nomme en français et en anglais tous les éléments de la plage qui sont présentés ici.

Say the name of each thing and find its picture in the book.

Prononce les mots que tu vois ici et
retrouve les éléments correspondants dans le livre.

| **waves** | **towel** | **shells** | **umbrella** |
| **des vagues** | **une serviette** | **des coquillages** | **un parasol** |